MUSICAL INSTRUMENTS

Text by
GIAMPIERO TINTORI

MAGNA BOOKS

The photographs contained in this volume were kindly contributed by:
Adriano Bacchella, Turin: fotos n° *41, 77;*
Photographic files of Lucchetti, Publishers: foto n° *60;*
Bissolotti Francesco, Cremona: fotos n° *64, 66;*
Collection of violins in the Palazzo Comunale in Cremona: foto n° *62;*
Monzino S.p.A., Lainate (Milan): fotos n° *4, 16, 79, 80, 81, 82;*
The Castle Museum, Milan: fotos n° *1, 2, 6, 7, 8, 24, 26, 28, 30, 32, 34, 37, 38, 39, 43, 44, 45, 46, 47, 49, 50, 52, 53, 54, 56, 57, 58, 68, 69, 70, 73, 75;*
Museum of the La Scala Theatre, Milan: fotos n° *3, 72;*
Prof. Romeo Orsi S.p.A., Buccinasco (Milan): fotos n° *11, 12, 13, 14, 18, 19, 20, 22;*

English translation by
JENNIFER PEARSON

Anthropologists have said that man is the only animal able to foresee the consequences of his actions, so he is the only one able to create a tool. Musical instruments are the greatest and most extraordinary tools that *homer faber* has managed to create, devising, via inert material, be this wood, metal or bone, a way of generating sound and the wonders that may result from a sound, or sounds put together in an appropriate way by the human mind.

The idea of cataloguing musical instruments is not a new one. The Chinese, to whom ancient inventions or ideas have often been attributed, have proposed picturesque classification of their creations according to material, the points of the compass, the seasons, the elements. For example, although drums belong, in terms of material, to the classification hide, they represent north, winter, water and so on.

Greek and Roman culture set down a classification which lasted through the Middle Ages, where, naturally, a more concrete trend was followed. Three main categories of instruments were established: percussion instruments (no distinction was made between idiophonic and membranophonic), wind instruments and string instruments. The first of the three were called Kroustikon by the Greeks, Pulsatile by the Romans and Percussionalia by people living in the Middle Ages. Wind instruments were called Pneumatikon by the Greeks, Inflatile by the Romans and Inflatilia during the Middle Ages. String instruments were respectively Enchordo, Tensile and Tensibilia.

As time went by, and various Mediaeval and Renaissance theories appeared, there was a greater and greater need for a precise classification which, at first sight, would not seem to present any particular problems. It is, however, a fact that unless classifications are carefully studied and tested, misunderstandings may arise.

We can give examples of this: the violin and the piano are string instruments, the organ has a keyboard like that of a piano but it works using air. Drums and xylophones are instruments which are struck but one is made of hide while the other is made of wood. In 1880 Victor Charles Mahillon, the founder of the extraordinary instrument museum of Brussels Conservatory proposed a classification based on the principle of acoustics, taking into account the nature of the object producing the sound. He thus established the following main categories: autophonic (later to be known as idiophonic), diaphragm, wind and string. This classification was perfected by Sachs and Horbonstel who added to the above a detailed list of subspecies (for example, instruments whose strings are plucked, string instruments played with a bow and those which function by the use of air etc).

The advent of Islamic culture had a profound effect on the development of instruments. It is only one of the reasons we are indebted to Islam, which is only too often linked to the idea of "infidels" without our ever realizing just how much it contributed to mathematics, astronomy and music.

Musicologist Henry George Farmer, in the chapter dedicated to Islam of his "History of the Music of Oxford", wrote, and rightly so, that Islamic civilization "is the greatest and most lasting contribution of any to be found in any culture between the Dark Ages and the Renaiscence". To confirm this affirmation it is enough to consider *Kitābu l Musīqī al Kabīr* (the great book on music by Abū Nasr al Fārābī, an Arabian sage who was born about 870 and died about 950. This Islamic scholar calculated, using mathematics, the positions of the fingers on the strings. As well as the important studies carried out by these theoreticians, collected in a valuable French translation by D'Erlanger and published in several volumes with the intervention of Farmer in the thirties, Islam has provided a contribution which has completely transformed our culture.

Until the advent of Islam, there was no knowledge of continuous sound on a string instrument. It was the followers of Islam who introduced instruments to be played with bows in the form of the *rebāb* (which was to become the Mediaeval rebeck) and the *kemānğela*, which involved both arm and leg; the lute with a small case and long neck and bent extremity. Unknown to our culture is the psaltery, a word taken from the Arab word *quānūn* (Mediaeval = cannon). When a keyboard is added to the psaltery we have the spinet, harpsichord and finally the piano, which is really just a large psaltery which instead of being plucked is struck with hammers.

The lute was to be the protagonist of the whole of Renaissance musical culture and was to survive even after the appearance of more convenient key instruments such as the arquelute, the theorbus and the large guitar. Indeed it was to continue its key role as witness (now at last becoming popular once more) to a great musical culture.

The violin is a perfect example of man's intelligence. From an immense variety of violas (arm, leg, amoroso, grand and so on) and hand held lutes (which show their Islamic ori-

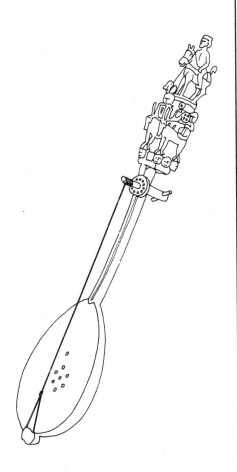

gins in their extremities with frontal pegs) luthiers have managed, with slow, relentless perseverence, to condense in four instruments played with bows all the characteristics of the original varieties. They combined in the violin (the violina or small violin) violas with a high tone, in the modern viola, violas with a medium tone, and in violincellos double-bass leg-supported violas, the latter, in turn, deriving from the Arabic words *kemānğe a' ğūz*. In addition the number of strings were reduced from six to four.

Musical instruments sometimes appear to possess qualities linked to certain peoples. The art of lute-making belongs to a great Italian tradition (while the French were the best at making bows); the piano (the old pianoforte created by Bartholomew Cristoforis) was traditionally Germanic; wind instruments are attributed to Belgian and French makers, while organs are the prerogative, above all, of the Italians and the French.

We have mentioned the history of musical instruments, and of course in the pages which follow we shall try and allow the reader to understand and learn to love what is one of man's greatest achievements. Surrounded as we are by the noise of city traffic, the roar of jet planes and assailed by the boom in computers, I feel that man, if he wishes to find the right equilibrium, without allowing himself to be seduced by what is only too often false progress, may with an instrument, in the tranquillity of his own room, discover worlds which he might never have dreamed existed.

1/2 — A column of air in a tube made of wood, as in this case, or other material, is stimulated in order to vibrate and produce a sound. If insufflation takes place directly, as in the straight flute (fig. 2), a slit to break the air is cut under the mouthpiece. In the clarinet (fig. 1) a reed is fixed to the mouthpiece. This piece of tubing, used with the correct technique by the player, will produce the required vibration.

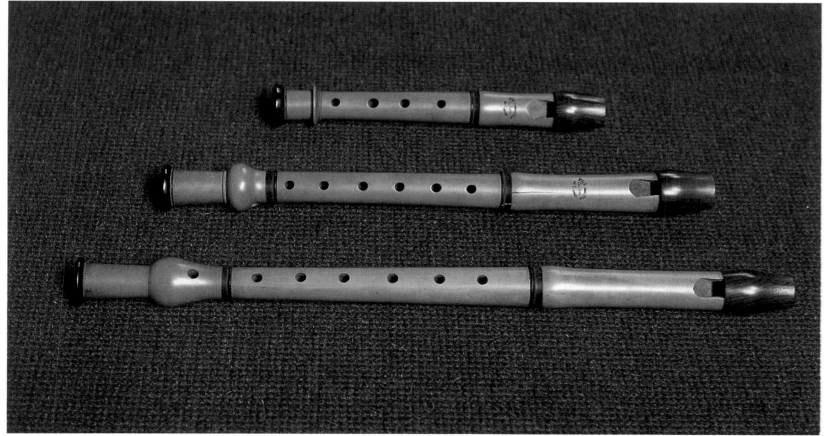

Opera Intitulata Fontegara
La quale isegna asonare di flauto cho tutta larte opportuna a esso istrumento
massime il diminuire il quale sara utile adogni istrumento di fiato er chorde: er achora a
chi si diletta di canto, coposta per sylvestro di ganassi dal fontego sonator d la Illma.Sa.D.V.

3 — Frontespiece of *Opera intitulata Fontegara*, by Silvestro di Ganassi Dal Fontego, Venice, 1535. As can be seen from the words above the scene, it is a manual or handbook for the straight flute or recorder.

4 — The straight flute or mouthpiece flute (German *Bockflöte*, English *Recorder*) was also called soft flute because of its characteristic sound. It is an ancient instrument and is part of a whole group, from the small soprano to the bass. The longer instruments, those with deeper sounds, have keys which enable the player to reach the fartner holes, the beginning of what was to be called the Böhm system during the first half of the nineteenth century.

5

5/8 — If the origins of the trumpet may be attributed to the shell or *Tritonium Variegatum*, then animal horns were the ancestors of the hunting horn, which was to acquire more virtue as it began to be used in orchestras. The horn (fig. 5) is an instrument with a curved tube or bore and conical outlet or bell, in which sound is produced by the vibration of the player's lips. The type of animal horn depends on the zone and the fauna living there: gazelle, antilope, oxen (fig. 7), elephant tusks (fig. 8). It is from the latter that the oliphant derived (fig. 6), that finely carved instrument that legend states was in the hands of Orlando, the Palatine Count and nephew of King Charles, who during his retreat from Spain, assailed by the Moors at Roncisvalle while he was in the rearguard and wanting to give news of this to the king, played it with such force that he split his temples in two.

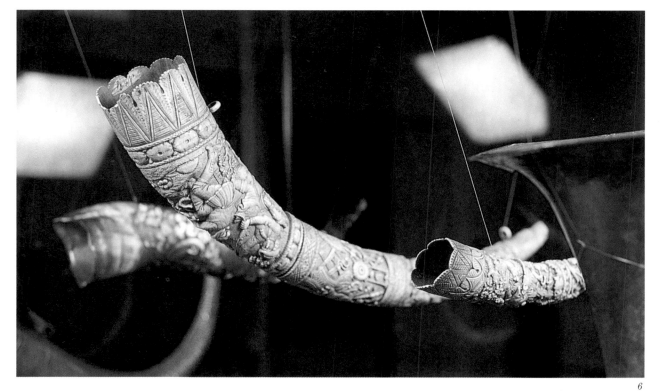

6

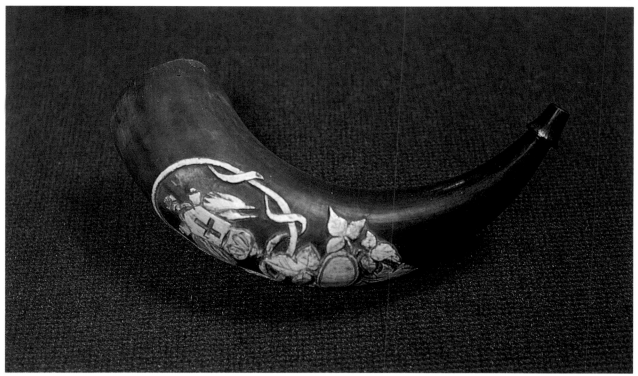

7

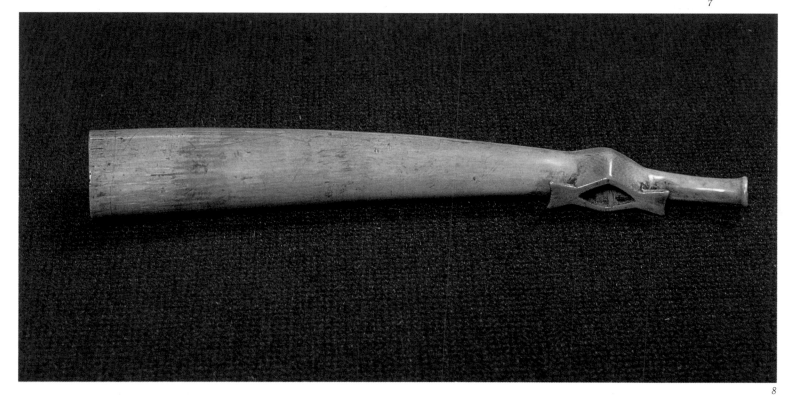

8

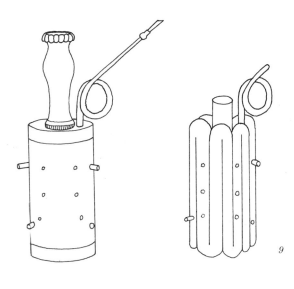

9

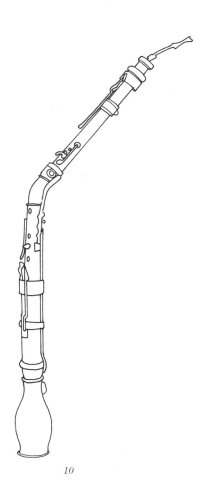

10

9/14 — The family of wood instruments has three types of insufflation: the direct insufflation of the transverse flute; the single reed of the clarinet mouthpiece (fig. 11); the double reed of the oboe, famous successor of the reed-pipe (fig. 12) and the bassoon with its long bent tube (fig. 14). The English horn, which produces the bass octave of the oboe (fig. 13) is not actually a horn and is not even English. It was called horn because of allusions to the first models with a curved tube, English by the reference to angled models (fig. 10). This appears to be an incorrect translation of *cor anglé*, read as *cor anglais*. There is also a small bassoon which contains the reed in a cylindrical box (fig. 9). The instrument, alluding to the tube which is rolled up like a sausage, has been given such strange names as *Wurstfagott* in German and *Cervelas* in French. It is also known as *Racket* and *Faustfagott*.

11

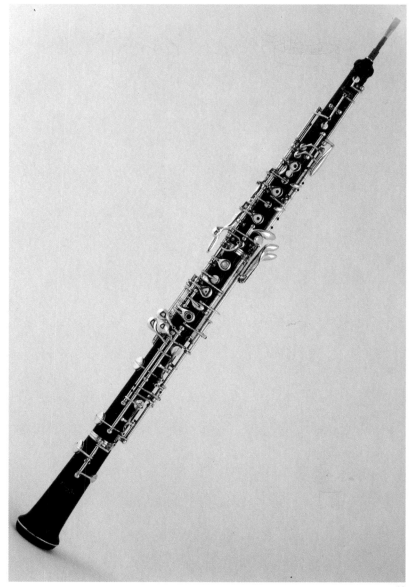

12

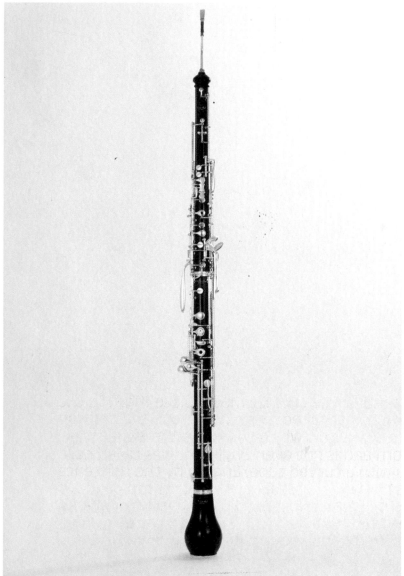

13

14

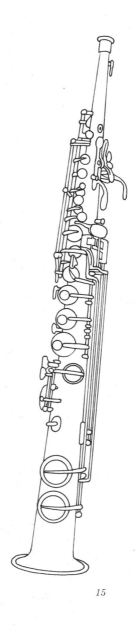

15

15/16 — The saxophone, with all the other instruments belonging to the same family (soprano, contralto, tenor, baritone, bass and double bass), was invented around 1840 in Brussels by Adolph Sax and the whole group was patented on 21st March 1846. Its original pipe-shaped form, evocative of the ancient Etruscan *Lituus*, has been modified for more acute sounds (fig. 15). Created to give bands more manageable instruments, with octaves and technically similar to the clarinet and able to fit in more easily than other instruments can, it has been cited, because of its charming and unusual sound, by Berlioz as "the most beautiful low voice known today". It became part of orchestras and was soon to be known as the typical instrument of jazz and small bands, thanks to its versatility.

17

17 — The cornet, a simple horn used in the Middle Ages as a hunting instrument and to give warnings, began to be used by military bands at the end of the eighteenth century. During the ages it has undergone no modifications worth noting. The cornet derives from the post-horn and the mellophone derives from the orchestral cornet which was part of military bands in the nineteenth century. The cornet is sometimes used in orchestras.

18/20 — Above the tenor saxophone (fig. 20) are two other members of the family of brass instruments: the trumpet (fig. 18) and the flicorno (flügelhorn) (fig. 19). Brass instruments use two types of bore; cylindrical for the trumpet and conical for the horn and its derivatives. Insufflation takes place through a cup-shaped mouthpiece. Before the invention of the piston, attributed to Friedrich Blühmel in 1813 and produced by Heinrich Stölzel in Berlin three years later, it was necessary to adapt the instrument to the tone of the piece being played by the retort, a U-shaped piece of tubing which was inserted, each time in a different size. The piston, with a simple pressure of the fingers, by diverting the air into a fixed device, varies the length of the tube, thus allowing an instrument made for only one tone to be used.
The cylindrical bore of the trumpet and the trombone produces a clear, sharp tone, the conical bore of the horn and other such instruments, a deeper tone.

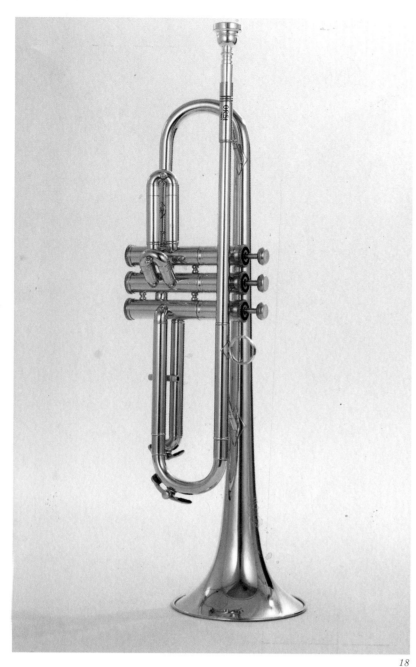

18

19

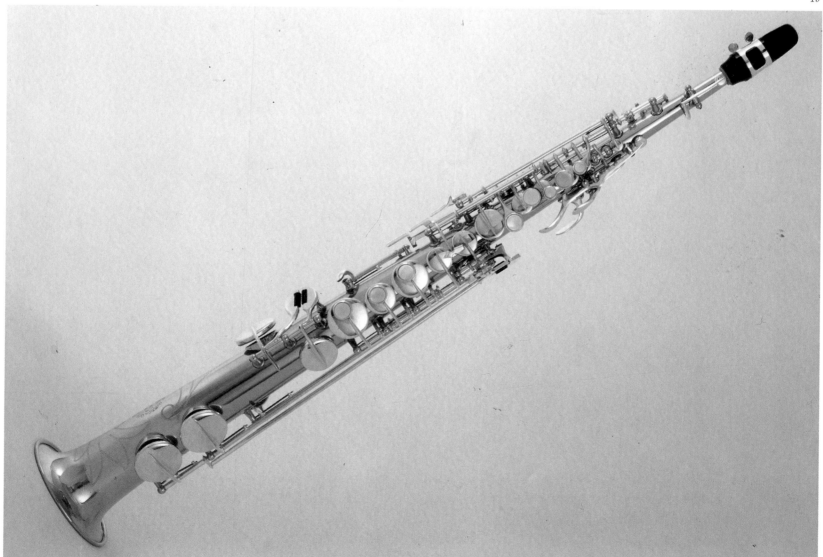

17

20

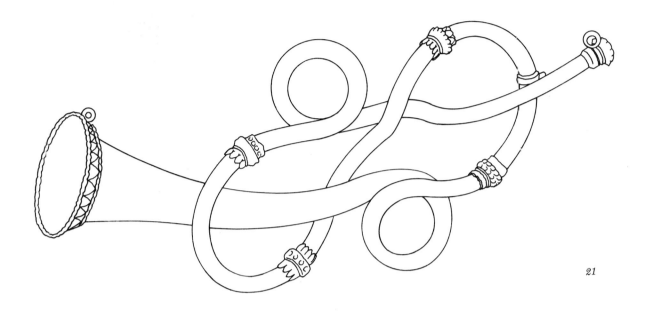

21

21 — The hunting horn, ancestor of the present-day horn, became part of orchestras during the second half of the eighteenth century, and Bach and Händel were to be its first enthusiastic supporters.

22 — The Fa horn used in orchestras, like other brass instruments, has spiral tubes which make it easy to handle (a modern horn has nearly six metres of tubing).

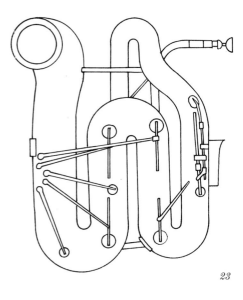

23

23/24 — The *serpentone* or coil cornet is a bass version of the ancient wooden cornet of octagonal shape, with a hide lining (known in German as *Zink*).

The oldest straight cornet may be seen in a Rhenish eleventh century miniature but the curved cornet became more widespread from the eighteenth to the nineteenth centuries. It too belonged to a large family, from the soprano downwards, and fell into disuse because of the difficulties involed in playing it. It was, however, used magnificently by Monteverdi in *Orfeus* when the Thracian singer found himself at the entrance to hell. The bass version (or coil cornet) survived (fig. 24) and was still used at the beginning of the century in French churches, despite Berlioz's comments that its sounds were "really barabaric, more suited to bloody Druid worship than the Catholic cult".

Fig. 23 shows an excellent example from the nineteenth century. It has a great many keys and massive structure.

25

25/26 — A beautiful "static" organ (fig. 26) which could not be moved, in contrast to the "portable" organ which can be played while taking part in processions. The organ used by the Romans at circuses for their absurd bloodthirsty games, of which Christians were so often the victims, was the only musical instrument used, up to a short time ago, in churches and is undoubtedly a symbol and reminder of those sacrifices.

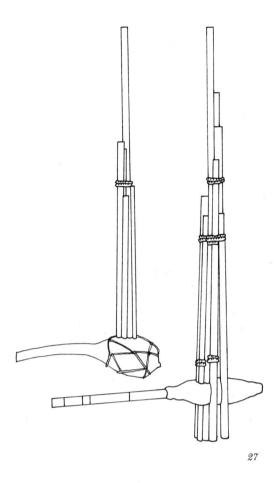

27

27/28 — A Chinese mouth-organ or *seng* (known in various forms in all countries of south-east Asia: in Korea as *saing*, in Japan as *sô*, in Burma as *Kien* and *fuku*, in Borneo as *kledi*). It is the prototype of our harmonium which was created when a *seng* was imported to St. Petersburg in the mid 1700s. The player inhales and blows alternately into a case or sound box to cause the small free-standing metal reeds to vibrate. These are located at the base of at least thirteen bamboo canes or tubes. The reeds are tuned by weighting them with a drop of wax and the fingers are placed over the holes. This instrument, used at funerals, fell into disuse because of the tiring effect on the player's lungs but it is still present, even though not always played, at funeral ceremonies.

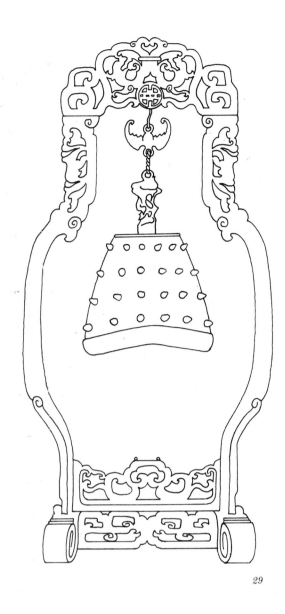

29

29 — Chimes which are rung by an external hammer have been known in China for nearly 400 years. They are found at the entrance to the residences of mandarins to announce visitors, ward off evil spirits during processions or drive away, during eclipses, the wicked dragon who is devouring the moon.

30 — The gong is a metal disc struck by a hammer. It is frequently found in south-east Asia and was known in China as far back as the sixth century A.D. The one shown in the illustration is used in the Japanese musical group known as *gagaku*. These bronze gongs are made in various sizes and are hung on decorated frames and struck with hard hammers. They are used to underline the stress in each phrase.

31

31/32 — The *darabukke* is a drum with a case made of decorated clay, but there are also models with cases made of wood or chiselled bronze. Very widespread in Islamic culture, this instrument has taken on many forms. The main body is held under the arm and the player strikes the sheep-hide with both hands.

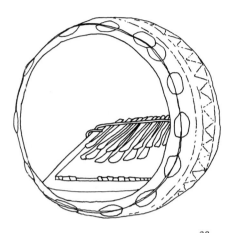

33

33/35 — The *zanza*, from a word meaning "the wood". It is an idiophonic instrument, played by plucking and well-known in African culture. It is widespread from the Congo to the coasts (fig. 34/35). When the instrument has metal parts, such as in the area along the banks of the Zambesi river, it is known as *nsimbi* "the iron". Some *zanzas* (fig. 33) also have a sound reverberating case made either of wood or a gourd.

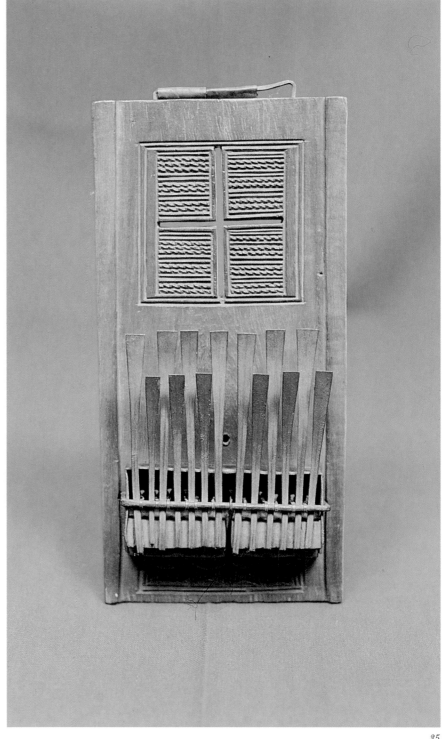

34

35

31

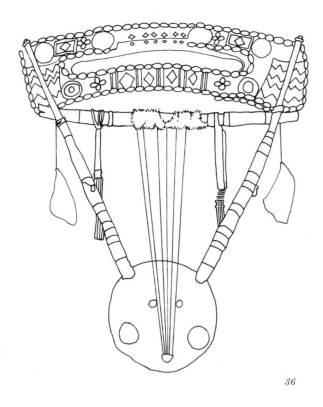

36

36 — An Ethiopian *kissar* with a bowl-shaped, highly-decorated case. The six strings depart from a ring fixed to the bottom of the case. Like the *bagana*, the *kissar* is played with a plectrum made of hide or from the claw of an animal, even though it is sometimes played just with the fingers.

37/38 — Two coïncidences, both as regards time and place, may easily be seen in these illustrations of an African harp or *nanga* (fig. 37) and a Burmese harp or *saun* (fig. 38), both identical in form. The African harp is, like all harps, a successor to the old musical bow and examples may be found of such dimensions that they cannot be placed between the thighs with the neck facing outwards, such as the *nedumu* of the Azandes, who claim to have invented an instrument which is placed on a stand. The Burmese harp, with its form similar to that of the ancient Eygptian harp and the *nanga* has led Curt Sachs to suppose that they all come from the same central Asian origins.

39 — The African lyre, *kissar*, an Ethiopian word deriving from the Greek κιθᾶρα (lyre).

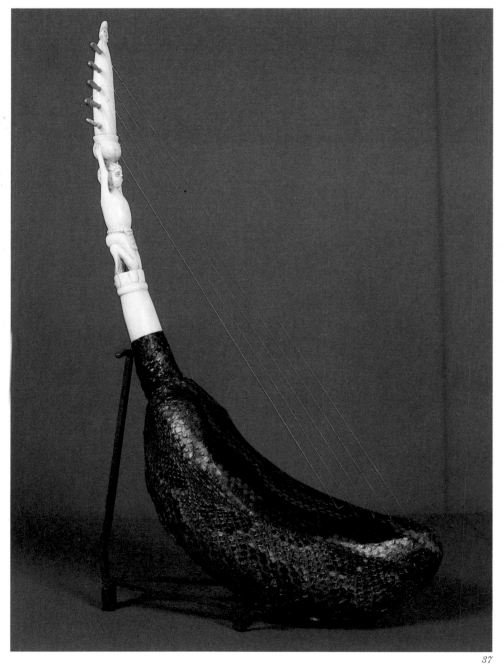

37

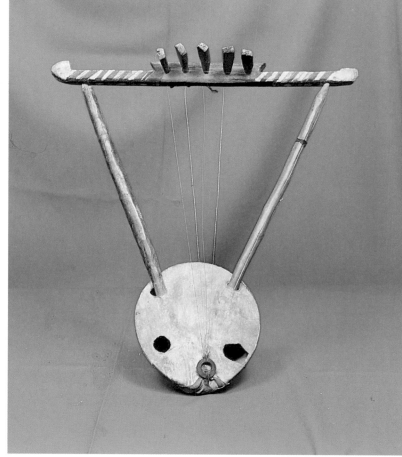

39

33

38

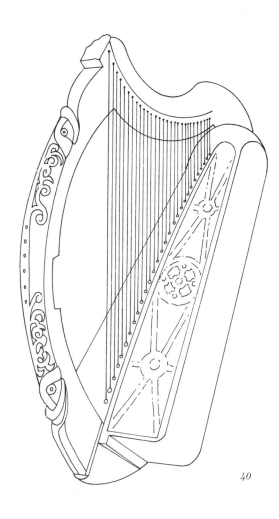

40

40/41 — The harp of King Brian Boru (fig. 40) who came to the throne of Ireland in 1001, now preserved in Dublin Museum and the first European example with a front column, this being absent in previous cultures. "This ancient instrument was brought from Ireland to us", wrote Vincenzo Galilei in *Dialogo sulla musica antica e moderna*, published in Florence in 1581. The harp later became widespread in Europe, keeping its basic structure intact while becoming bigger and adopting the new contruction techniques thought up by Cousineau in 1782 and Erard in 1790 (fig. 41). They added pedals, first two rows with one notch, then two rows with two notches for each pedal, so that, acting on a series of strings reached by stretching the arms, the pedal, with a system of discs, gave two types of tension, raising notes by a semi-tone or a tone.

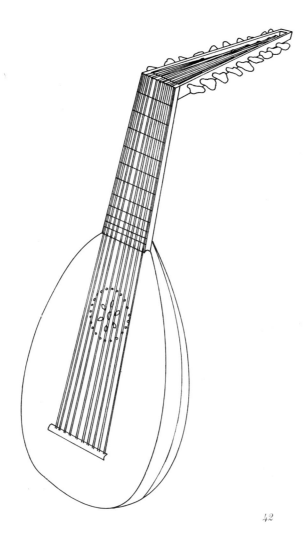

42

42/47 — *El lud*, the wood. This was the name given by Islam to what was to become our lute (fig. 42), the splendid Renaiscence instrument. The Chinese lute (fig. 43) is called *p'i p'a* (In Japanese *biwa*). It has a finger-piece which also continues on the board. On the upper part of the handle are ivory triangles which, by moving the fingers over the catheti, create small variations of a quarter tone which are typical of the musical systems of the Far East (and which were also used in ancient Greece). From China too comes the *yüeh k'in* (fig. 44), the "moon guitar", suitable for serenades, and finally the *samisen* (fig. 45) used in Japan exclusively by women.
In the next row is the *balalaika* (fig. 46), with its typical triangular case, probably of Tartar origin and widespread all over Russia during the 1700s. It comes in six sizes: from the small (sharp) to the large double bass. Finally a Turkish folk string instrument (fig. 47) which, if it were not for the long neck, could belong to the same family as the Italian mandolin.

43

44

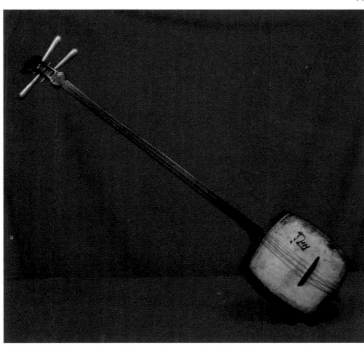

45

46

47

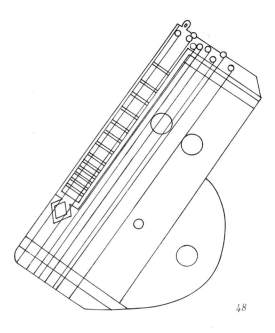

48

48/50 — The fundamental contribution of Islam to our culture included, among other things, the *quanün*, the Arab psaltery which was to have, with the introduction of the keyboard, extraordinary consequences and bring us to the piano. The psaltery is known in all cultures, from China to Europe where, at present, only three types have survived: the Russian *gusli*, the Hungarian percussion *cymbalon* and the Tyrolean *zither*. Illustrated here are: a splendid western psaltery dating back to the seventeenth century (fig. 49), a Japanese psaltery or *koto* (fig. 50) which, by varying the name and adding other features may have from one to fifty strings. Fig. 48 shows a Yugoslavian psaltery.

49

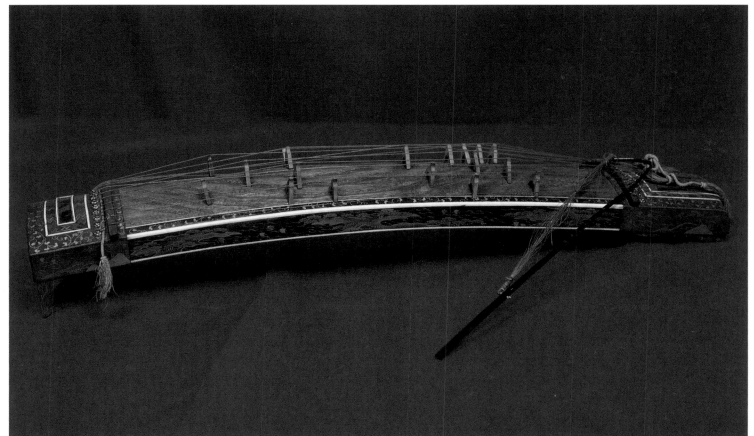

50

39

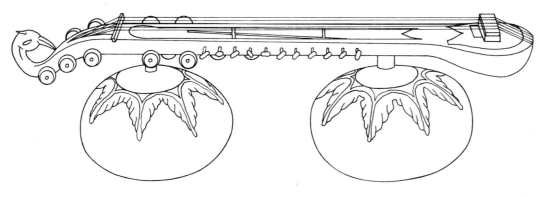

51

52

53

54

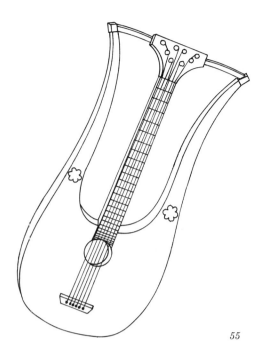

55

55/56 — The guitar as we know it today derives from the Spanish *guitara* (fig. 56), even though the basic structure is very old and can even be traced back as far as Egyptian and Hittite civilizations. The guitar has been of interest to all social classes, with noble, exquisitely carved and decorated instruments, and has also played the role of folk instrument (a model with a very deep case known as *chitarra battente* is popular in Calabria) and was used to enliven the merry groups of people gathered in taverns. It was made also in special shapes, such as the lyre-guitar (fig. 55).

57 — The mandolin, a direct descendant of the lute.

58 — An elegant *tiorbino*, a reduced version of the normal *thecrbo*, a member of the ar- quelute family, with an added anklepiece for the strings not played outside the neck. The inlay work on the handle is very pretty and delicate.

56

57

58

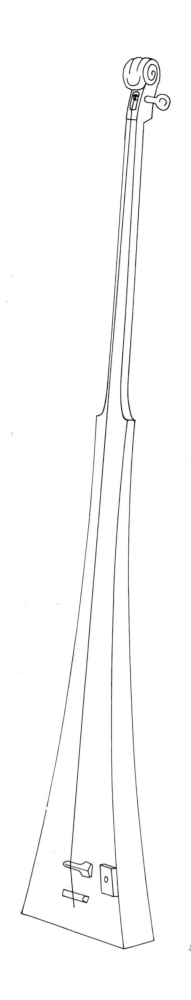

59

59 — A *tromba marina* (marine trumpet), which is neither a trumpet nor has anything to do with the sea but is so called as it was used by nuns (the trumpet of Maria) as a substitute for the regular trumpet used to give signals in monasteries and which was not considered fitting for a nun. Played with a double bass bow and finger movements producing harmonious sounds, it produced a real blare of sound.

60 — *Still life with musical instruments.* Evaristo Baschenis (1617-1677). Several instruments used during the Baroque period are depicted here: the violin, the viola, the straight flute, the *mandora* and the lute.

60

61

61/62 — A violin by Antonio Stradivarius (fig. 62), the great luthier of the Cremona school, perhaps an apprentice at that time but certainly a follower of the art of Nicolò Amati, descendant of Andrea, who inspired the Cremona school. In the preface mention is made of the wonderful synthesis that the luthiers created from the numerous, even confusing family of violas. Using only one basic model they devised, in four types (fig. 61), the modern string quartet.

62

63

63/64 — The viola (fig. 63) was for many years the Cinderella of the orchestra, assuming roles such as assisting the bass instruments or providing harmonic undertones.
It has an ingenious paladin in Hector Berlioz who wrote the fascinating musical work *Aroldo in Italia*. The instrument we see illustrated here below (fig. 64) is the work of the Cremonese luthier Franfesco Bissolotti and was made for Salvatore Accardo.

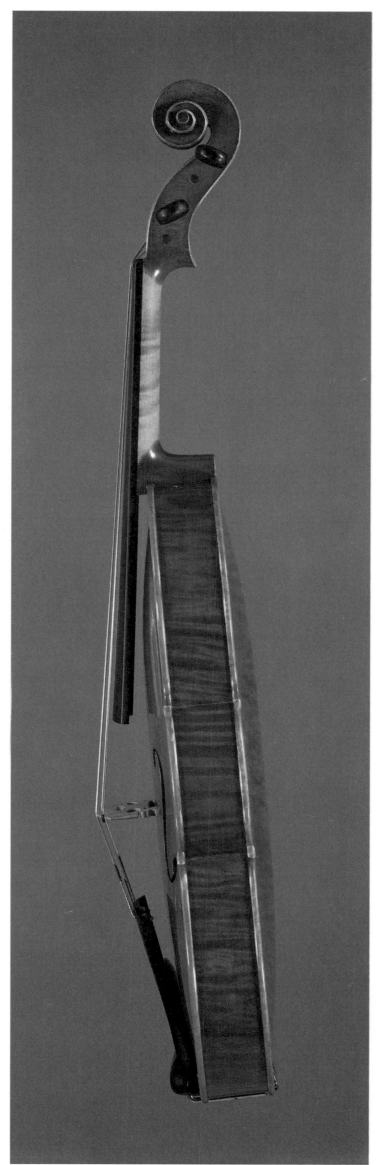

49

65

65 — The leg-supported lyre, or large lyre, was a bass version of the hand-held lyre, which in turn, derived from the *fidula* around the end of the 1400s. It had from nine to fourteen main strings and two strings outside the neck, used for undertones. Besides the usual sound holes it could also have a carved central hole.

66 — Despite the important modifications carried out by Luigi Boccherini, the violincello had a hard time making itself accepted. Indeed, in 1740 in Amsterdam Le Blanc published a further pathetic piece in defence of the bass viola. The instrument shown here is another creation of Francesco Bissolotti's.

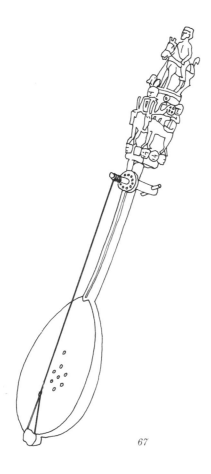

67

67/68 — The Yugoslavian *gusli*, as Yiarte, a nineteenth century traveller and explorer wrote, hangs on the walls of inns, just as the Spanish guitar and *pandero* (tambourine) hang on the walls of the posada (tavern). It is a folk instrument, popular with the old ballad singers who would accompany their song with the *gusli*.

69 — Bows of various periods and types. The fourth from the left is interesting as it has a ring into which the finger was inserted to stretch the hairs, before the introduction of the modern screw version.

70 — The hurdy-gurdy, a string instrument which works by friction. The handle turns a pitch-coated wheel which rubs on the strings, the side ones used for undertones (not pressed, so having a continuous sound). Instead those inside the neck case are touched by small black and white protruding parts. The hurdy-gurdy was also called blind man's viola or crutch. As it was easy to handle, it was played by blind men who also used it as a walking-stick (as in the famous painting by Jeronimus Bosch). The French called it *viele a roue*, the Gremans *Drehleier*. It was well-known in the Middle Ages, mentioned by the ancient name of *organistrum* by Odo de St. Maur-des-Fosses (who died in about 1030 A.D.) in a text attributed to Odo de Cluny.

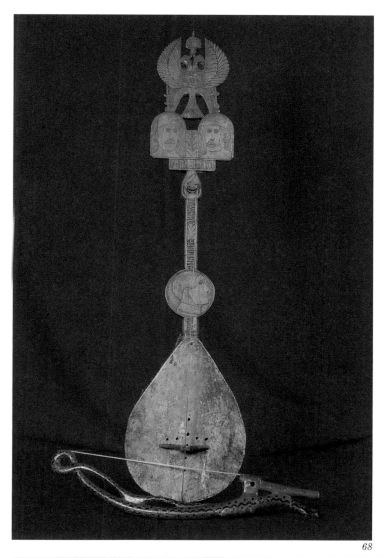

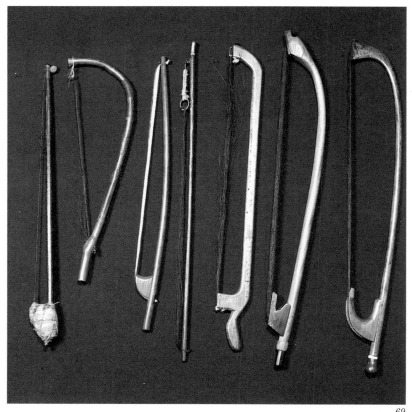

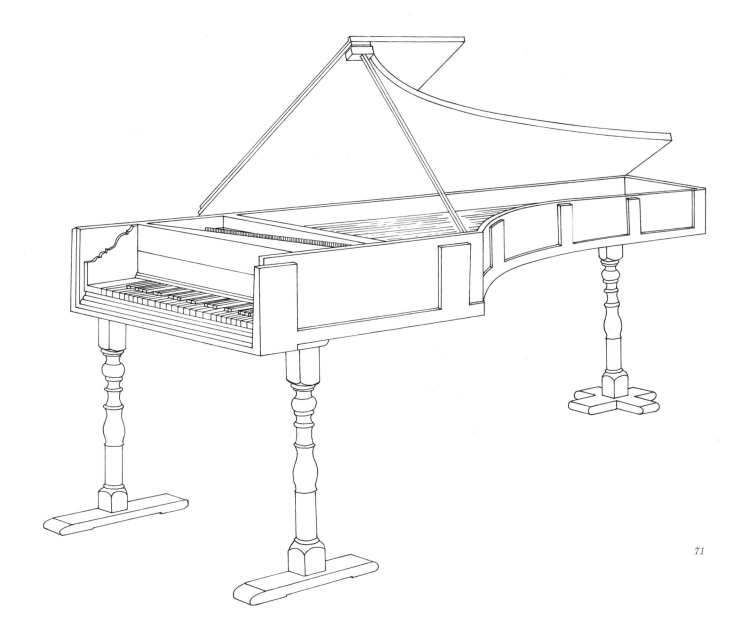

71

71 — The revolutionary invention of Bartolomeo Cristofori, the *forte-piano*, in which the nib-shaped strikers of the harpsichord were substituted with hammers, thus obtaining various degrees of intensity of sound without having to use regulators. There are only three of Cristofori's forte-pianos left: one dating back to 1720, the one shown here from 1722 and one dated 1726.

72 — Model C Steinway piano, with three patents. The tone pedal was perfected by and the echo device studied in collaboration with the famous physicist Hermann Ludwig Ferdinand von Helmholtz. Made in 1882 in New York, it was sent to Hamburg and presented in 1883 to Franz Liszt, who considered it an excellent instrument. Now, after several misadventures, it is in the La Scala theatre museum and has recently been restored.

73 — A beautiful spinet, which derived from the addition of a keyboard to the ancient psaltery.

74

74/75 — The «giraffe» piano (fig. 75) along with the Viennese pyramid-shaped piano dating back to about 1820. These were the first experimental models aimed at reducing the space required by the grand piano, experiments which were to bring about the advent of the upright piano. This became popular in middle-class nineteenth century homes which no longer had the spaciousness of the royal residences and stately homes of the eighteenth century.

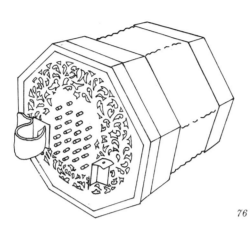

76

76/77 — *Accordeons* (fig. 76) and accordions (fig. 77) are instruments with free-standing tongues invented at the beginning of the XIXth century. They have a keyboard at one end linked to a bellows which directs air over the tongues. The simplest models have few buttons or have keys like those of a piano keyboard while the accordeons and accordions used by professional players are complex instruments able to execute music pieces of various types.

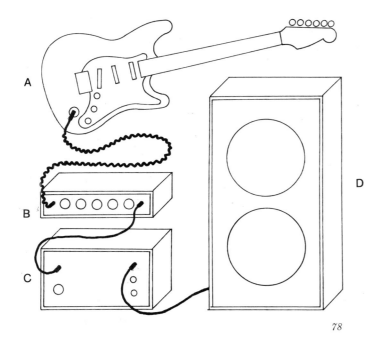

A

B

C

D

78

78 — Blueprint of an electric guitar. The vibrations of the strings are converted by the reproducer (a) into electrical impulses. These pass through the preamplifier (b) which has regulators for tone and volume (c) before reaching the speakers (d).

79 — Compact-case electric guitar by Yamaha. This type of instrument was created by Gibson for Les Paul. In the electric guitar the case or sound box serves only as a support for the strings and theoretically the instrument could do without it. In fact the quality of the sound is determined by electrical components and amplification.

80/81 — Two models of Yamaha digital synthesizers. The frontal panel (fig. 80) includes controls for the oscillators, mixing devices, filters, amplifiers and other control systems usually worked by a keyboard. Synthesizers like the one shown here have an electronic programming device able to control each aspect of sound production: pitch, length of the note, rhythm and volume. The various controls allow the musician to simulate the sound of traditional instruments.

82 — The set of drums was originally created by joining a series of single modern drums used by dance orchestras and jazz bands. This included: military drum, reverberating drum, large drum, three single cymbals and a pair of cymbals worked by a foot pedal. As may be seen, the new needs of contemporary music have caused it to become bigger and bigger, until it has reached the large proportions of the one shown.

82

Printed in Italy
in october 1990
by G.E.P. - Cremona - Italy